HENRY KNOWS BEST!

A STORY ABOUT LEARNING FROM MISTAKES AND LISTENING TO OTHERS

Written by Emily Learing, LMFT, RPT-S

Illustrated by Denise Turu

Henry Knows Best!
A Story About Learning from Mistakes and Listening to Others

Copyright© 2021 by Emily Learing

All rights reserved. No part of this book may be copied or reproduced in any manner whatsoever or in any format—written or electronic—without written permission from the copyright owner, except as permitted by U.S. copyright law.

For permissions, contact:
Beans & Bear Press, LLC
Attn: Emily Learing
Emily@BeansAndBearPress.com

Written by Emily Learing
Cover Design and Illustrations by Denise Turu
Photography by Anna Kroil Images

ISBN: 978-1-7367445-1-2
Library of Congress Control Number: 2021904643

Publisher's Cataloging-in-Publication data

Names: Learing, Emily, author. | Turu, Denise, 1976-, illustrator.
Title: Henry knows best ! a story about learning from mistakes and listening to others / written by Emily Learing, LMFT, RPT-S ; illustrated by Denise Turu.
Description: Sioux Falls, SD: Beans & Bear Press, LLC, 2021. | Summary: After a day of rejecting others' advice, Henry realizes he does not always know best, and that his choices have consequences for himself and others.
Identifiers: LCCN: 2021904643 | ISBN: 978-1-7367445-1-2 (hardcover) | 978-1-7367445-0-5 (paperback) | 978-1-7367445-2-9 (ebook)
Subjects: LCSH Emotions in children--Juvenile fiction. | Decision making--Juvenile fiction. | Family--Juvenile fiction. | Dogs--Juvenile fiction. | CYAC Emotions in children--Fiction. | Decision making--Fiction. | Family--Fiction. | Dogs--Fiction. | BISAC JUVENILE FICTION / Social Themes / Emotions & Feelings | JUVENILE FICTION / Social Themes / Manners & Etiquette | JUVENILE FICTION / Family / General | JUVENILE FICTION / Animals / Dogs
Classification: LCC PZ7.1.L3926 Hen 2021 | DDC [E]--dc23

Published by Beans & Bear Press, LLC
Printed in Sioux Falls, SD

This is a book of fiction based upon a pet of the author and copyright owner of this book. Any resemblance to actual persons or animals—living or dead—events or locales is entirely coincidental.

To Beans and Bear, my motivation to make the world a better place.

To my husband, the man who has believed in and supported me since the day we met.

To my parents, who always dreamed I would write a children's book, and—*more importantly*—believed that I could.

–EL

A Note to the Caregiver

As a parent or teacher, you know just how difficult it can be to teach important life lessons to someone who thinks he or she always knows best! Whether you are raising a strong-willed child, have a child going through a very confident and independent stage, or have a classroom full of *"I know best"* kind of thinking, *Henry Knows Best!* can help you to start valuable conversations with the children in your life about how to become their best self by learning from mistakes and growing from the advice that others have to share.

The idea for Henry came from my very own strong-willed child *(of the canine variety)* — a corgi who is loved deeply by his family but who experiences some challenges in life due to his strong-willed personality. I created him so that you will have a more comfortable way to start talking with the children in your life about the importance of learning from mistakes and from the advice of others, while together you experience a day in the life of an adorable, strong-willed corgi.

As you read *Henry Knows Best!* with the children in your life, I encourage you to utilize some of the suggestions below to help them to see the impact of Henry's actions—*on himself and others*—to ensure that Henry's story helps their understanding of how strong wills can impact life and relationships.

Consequences

Henry Knows Best! was written to specifically emphasize consequences. As you read this book together, take time to pause and look at all of the consequences—*positive and negative*—that Henry experiences on this particular day to help children to understand the impact of unnecessary strong-willed behavior. I have specifically left sections of this book without text to allow the illustrations to show the full consequences of Henry's actions. Take this as an opportunity to really dive into the scene and talk about what happened as a result of Henry's choices.

Influences

One of the challenges that strong-willed personalities like Henry face is that they almost always think that only they have the most value to share in a situation. They aren't trying to be self-centered or boastful; they are just born to think that their way is the best way. As a result, they may fail to learn from the value that others have to share. As you read this book, take note of the value that each of the influencers had on Henry's day. While reading, or after you finish the book, talk about what value Henry missed out on by not listening to the suggestions of the positive influencers in the story.

Love & Importance

Parents and caregivers are often concerned that kids with a strong-willed personality are going to be viewed in a negative light. They want to help their strong-willed child to learn how to be more agreeable, but they don't want to crush their spirit in the process. As you read this book, pay special attention to the loving undertones of those who offer guidance and correction to Henry. Note that they give him advice to help him because they care for him and want him to do well in life, not just to boss him around and tell him what to do. Note how Henry's mom has a loving, connected moment with him after a long day of poor choices, versus a negative power struggle. As you read together, be sure to talk about the love that Henry's mom shows to him to help support children in knowing that they are loved too, even if they have moments—*few or many*—of thinking that only they know best.

- Emily Learing, LMFT, RPT-S

CONFIDENT Henry thinks that he **ALWAYS** knows best.
Every morning he wakes up and puffs up his chest
And tells those who cross him **ONLY** he knows the way
To solve **EVERY** problem he'll be faced with that day.

So his mom, dad and teacher who **LOVE** him and **CARE**,
Try to teach him to **LISTEN** and **LEARN** to be fair.

And some days Henry listens and gets through the day
Without getting in **TROUBLE** or **HURT** in some way.
But today, Henry forgot his listening ears,
And it resulted in some **HURT FEELINGS** and **TEARS**.

When his mom said, *"Henry, that's not where that toy goes!"*
Henry said, *"**I KNOW BEST!**"* while he turned up his nose.

With a **CRASH** and a **BANG**, his toys fell to the ground
And broke into pieces;
Some may **NEVER** be found.

A bit later today, his dad said with a smile,
"If you want to make friends, let **THEM** *talk for a while."*

"*He's not right...***I KNOW BEST***,*" Henry thought, looking proud.
So he just kept on talking, this time **EXTRA LOUD!**

Then, when his brother shared what he wanted to play,
Henry **TURNED OFF HIS EARS** to what he had to say.

"My idea is **BETTER**," he said, puffing his chest.
"You may not know it yet, but **I ALWAYS KNOW BEST!**"

So, later tonight, as Henry crawled into bed,
His mom placed a small kiss on the top of his head.

You must know it's my job to **TEACH** you as you grow,
And to tell you all the things in life you must know.

"I was **WORRIED**, my love, each time I watched you play.
It seems you didn't learn any lessons today.
Whenever you were offered somebody's advice,
You refused to listen...and then **YOU PAID THE PRICE!**"

"There are others in life who have value to share:

Your dad,

Grandparents,

Teachers,

And others **WHO CARE**."

"They just want to **HELP** because they care about you,
Not to boss you around or tell you what to do."

"Of course, I do," he said, snuggling into her chest,
"Because mom, don't you know that **I ALWAYS KNOW BEST?**"

*"Today, you showed me that you do not understand
Much about what it takes to become a good friend.*

The most wonderful friends know how to **COMPROMISE**.*"*
His mom pulled him in close and looked into his eyes.

"Can you do that, my love? Understand when you're **WRONG?**
When you do, it shows others you truly are strong."

"Yes mom, I can," Henry said. "I really will **TRY**.
But it is hard for me. Do you want to know why?"

I really do think **ONLY** I know what to do.
It's hard to admit there are others who do too!

Oh Henry, my love, it's OK to feel that way.
I, too, forget to listen to what others say.

"Just keep this in mind, dear, as you learn and you grow.
With **PRACTICE**, it becomes something you just learn to know.
Today is just one day. There are many ahead.
You have time to **LEARN** and practice all I've just said."

"For now though, Henry, it's just time to rest."
"Hey mom," Henry said, "I guess tonight, **YOU KNOW BEST!**"

EMILY LEARING - AUTHOR

Emily is a Licensed Marriage and Family Therapist and Registered Play Therapist Supervisor who works with children and their parents in play therapy at her counseling practice, and a blogger for parents of *strong-willed children*. Emily became inspired to write *Henry Knows Best!* after years of hearing parents of strong-willed children share their stories about their attempts to encourage more cooperative behavior in their child without crushing their child's spirit in the process. Emily used her first-hand experience working with these parents to create a loveable, strong-willed character that children can connect with and learn from to help and support parents of strong-willed children as they try to accomplish this goal. When she's not helping children and their parents, she's at home with her husband, two sons and two corgis. You guessed it…one of them is a strong-willed corgi named Henry! For tips, lots of empathy and support during the journey of raising a strong-willed child, visit Emily's blog at DisciplinedChildren.com.

DisciplinedChildren.com

DENISE TURU - ILLUSTRATOR

Denise studied Visual Arts in Buenos Aires, Argentina. From a very young age, she participated in various art exhibitions for children. In 2000, she won a painting contest in New York City, which led her to move and live there for 7 years. Her work was exhibited at the *Argentine Embassy in* New York, *Art Gallery 216 in* Soho *and S.e.e.d Gallery in* Brooklyn. Denise also worked as a set designer and as a mural painter for private clients in Manhattan, The Hamptons and Long Island. In 2007 she left New York City and for 6 years lived in different European cities (Barcelona, Dublin, Paris and London). She held various residencies and exhibitions throughout Europe. In 2008, she published her first graphic novel about her life, *A Custom-made map*. In 2013, she settled in Barcelona. The birth of her twins inspired her to work as an illustrator for children's books, including: *Babbit & Joan, Abecedario de Peces Imaginarios, Dinosaur Devotions* and many more. She currently lives in Barcelona and works worldwide.

deniseturu.com

WHO IS HENRY?

Henry is a floppy-eared, strong-willed, Tri-Colored Pembroke Welsh Corgi who is at his happiest when a generous soul offers to rub his belly. While no one knows exactly why his ear is floppy, his family believes it is one of his most lovable qualities.
When he's not showing his owners that he knows best by ignoring requests and moving at the speed of molasses in January whenever he's asked to do something, he enjoys walks —although he prefers riding in a stroller—pouncing in snow drifts and doing everything in his power to prevent his corgi brother from entering his domain of the house.

Henry hopes that his beloved strong-willed character will help children around the world to understand the importance of learning from their mistakes and listening to others. He's so glad that you decided to share his story with the children in your life!

CPSIA information can be obtained
at www.ICGtesting.com
Printed in the USA
BVHW020951181121
621924BV00005B/180